High-Frequency READERS™

W9-AZH-946

We Like Fruit

Written by Millen Lee
Illustrated by Tungwai Chau

Scholastic Inc.
New York   Toronto   London   Auckland   Sydney
Mexico City   New Delhi   Hong Kong

No part of this publication may be reproduced in whole or in part, or stored in a retrieval system, or transmitted in any form or by any means, electronic, mechanical, photocopying, recording, or otherwise, without written permission of the publisher. For information regarding permission, write to Scholastic Inc., Education Group, 555 Broadway, New York, NY 10012.

ISBN 0-439-13990-2

Copyright © 1999 by Scholastic Inc. All rights reserved. Published by Scholastic Inc. SCHOLASTIC and associated logos are trademarks and/or registered trademarks of Scholastic Inc.

10 19 18

8 9/0
23

Printed in the U.S.A.

First Scholastic clubs printing, November 1999

We go to the store.

I like apples and oranges.

I like oranges and pears.

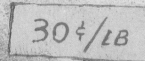

I like pears and peaches.

Peac

5

I like peaches and bananas.

I like bananas and strawberries.

We like fruit.